Syllables of Night
Joshua C. Welsch

Windwood Hill Press

2014

Introduction

After I have had a really awful day, I always take a moment - or if I am lucky, an entire evening, - to sit out on my porch. Often times, I will begin around late afternoon, so I can view the sky shifting from the light blue of summer sky into an inky, starlit blackness. I watch the trees, at first alive and textured and distinct, slowly becoming cloaked in darkness, until I can only see their impressions against the horizon. It is at this time, when I can no longer look at the grass and trees around me, that I look inward. Images of the day replay in my head - the choices made, the people met, the regrets of the past and the hopes of the future. It is in this contemplative state that I am able to see exactly where I am and where I want to be. This gives me the guidance in the days to come, to make the choices that would do best to others and to myself.

I think this effect that the atmosphere of night has on me relates to the very concept of existence. As human beings, we are endlessly rooted to a cycle - cycles of morning and evening, the changing seasons, birth and death. One might think that these cycles would become boring after a while, but the human experience is quite to the contrary. When spring arrives it is regarded with happiness, an excuse to shake off the drudgery of winter. And yet, in the same breath, there is a sense of sadness that the festivities and snow and frost-tightened hugs of winter have gone. The birth of a child is celebrated with the same degree of joy and wonder that is expressed in grief at the death of a loved one. Birth and death, spring and winter, morning and night - these are not anything new to us. But that does make them any less captivating.

So here, in this book, I am touching everything that has been in my cycle thus far. These reflections of nighttime cover an array of emotions and concepts that I have felt at some point. Love, disillusionment, abandonment, contradiction, contentedness, doubt and failure are all apart of me, and they are all here. But the most comforting thing for me to think about is that my cycle is nowhere near its end, giving me many more hours to watch the night.

Table of Contents

Good-bye	9
Molly: in memory of 1948	11
Ode	13
The Claim of Death	15
Growing	17
Vision	19
The Singer	21
The Pledge	23
Hermit's Manifesto	25
Untitled [pain in the night]	27
Accomplishment	29
Last Moment	31
Community	33
What Matters	35
Untitled [I miss you every day]	37
First Leaf	39
Trout	41
Estranged	43
Thoughts of Morning	45
Cult-ure	47
Frame	49
Flowers	51
Words	53
Failure	55
--------------	57
On you surrounded by my friends who I do not know	59
Slave	61
Cross	63
Untitled [Are we all dying?]	65
Widowed Chapel	67
Untitled	69
Evolution of Separation	71

Meditation	73
Funeral (of a grandmother)	75
Night-time	77
Orange	79
Seventh Realm	81

Good-by

I say goodnight as the sun rises

To the trembling realities and friendships and secrets

As the time which we shared with the rhythms of table tennis

And gentle conversations on deep doubts that plague us as we lie in bed at night

Disappear into our building of past experiences

Where picture frames on walls show precious moments

Which we put there to keep from losing them and becoming lost

And stare at them, to hold the emotions that we felt

Already the pictures are changing.

Molly: in memory of 1948

In a room full of shadow a piano sits

Lonely and old in the moonlight, touching its slender keys

If only for a moment shines the deepest longing

That sits and hums inside your chest

Playing a waltz, and the house is sunshine

With golden liquid and laughter from everywhere

A roaring fire a warm couch a cat curled up, sleeping contentedly

The friends are many and merry,

But the waltz comes to an end.

The pause between notes tells us this is something indeed; growing moving forward into what we knew had to be there. The future is a darkness where anything can happen.

Cover your eyes and it might not exist.

The claps for the musician fade away into the single candle illuminating the room

Dusty furniture and glassware for better times

The room is empty and cold aside from you and the piano.

Wind tearing at the house asking you to play just once more,

No no, you say.

Not tonight.

Ode

What if I told you
I never wanted to write
The walls of my consciousness
Across your membrane papyrus
Crafted from the whispering wind
Sown between the leaves?

Would you envelope yourself in the endless ashes of history
Lose yourself in the oceans of forgotten memory
Forlorn words wandering as I sleep
Locking the door of my longing in the rhythms of my breath, a wind
Pushing you from my threshold
Giving you no home

Sending you out into the night
Taking the only piece of pride you clung to
The warm shawl of a name.

The Claim of Death

When I sit in bed
I feel like curling up
Into a tight little ball
And dying.

Shrink away from the world
Become lost in sheets which
Will never be as white
As a coffin's rich intestines
Or the after life
After death

It's funny
We get squeezed into this world like a cannonball wreaking havoc
And settling in some far off field
Of daises and lilies

Why should we rest when so few of our actions grant us the right of death?

Keep those too afraid to
Give their lives to something
On a ventilator breathing rhythmically
In endless sleep.

<u>Growing</u>

Speak softly in black imagination
Images stretched across ceilings and walls.
Of experiences once seen through dreams as young children
Where everything was everything we knew and
Our own universe of how things go
Was nothing that you couldn't find in books of happilyeverafters.
This we glimpse in cold
Dark around midnight with nothing to ask
But when will light shine through these shades
And give these yearnings skin?

Vision

Creaking of the boat
As the gentle rocking of a mother
Soothes through the deepest fears
And the patterned membranes of the sea,
Through the catastrophe of wake and waves,
I find a reason
Looking out to the line of where the sea meets the sky,
Vague memories in the grayness of the fog
Blend with the detailed patterns, through which there is no escape
And form I to me

The Singer

As he stood in front of the reflecting lights
His eyes were closed and his mouth was open
In the gasp and breath of a beautiful cry
I couldn't see the space and time
Flowing through, swaying the whole room.

The Pledge

Feeble, I know you.
When you leapt upon the grass. And the flowers bloomed
Years passed, and underneath petunias and sycamores,
I profess, profess, profess my love.
And drying in the sun, I lie down
On the pavement, a pool for the senses,
and I didn't care how I looked, or what I did.
(Mirrors were invisible to me)
And I felt underneath a pink, soft light, a cheek, a nose, a smile.
Pity, our eyes memory, and we blind the beauty of the past.
The flowers blossoming in the courtyard.

Hermit's Manifesto

most times
im a fish
putting gigantic
glassbowl projections
in perspective
as the shapes
stretch and blur
i wait for something
resembling an impression of myself

i have never seen my own reflection.

Untitled [pain in the night]

The cars pass in the pain of the night.
When the lamps are set for oiling again,
Toiling against the dark which rages inside
On the brink where only words are held trembling to gather strands
Screaming thought after thought of things
you would never whisper in the hand of day

(A small child stands alone. It is in rags and is bleeding from its arms and face. Its mouth is open, screaming out, but the music is too loud. Suddenly the child vanishes, replaced by total silence.)

What do you cling to when all things are gone

Accomplishment

i told myself
i wanted to write
a poem of despair
something awash in loss
pain and loneliness, true enough
to make the rich man uneasy
and the holy man weep.

then I realized
that it was all meaningless anyway
and turned over
facing the wall.

Last Moment

the end of the world will be
a flick of a switch
and all is darkness

God needs a break too, you know
and screw nightlights

Community

even though I am
surrounded by trees
i still feel
lonely
in a city

maybe because
it is pitch black
and I am wandering
in a sea of ghosts
who do not know my name

What Matters

the familiar ache when I think of you
runs through me at the times

when I can think of nothing else
and the philosophy I kept on the counter top

is dull, the questions of humanity gone
in some mist in the palm of your hand which

you show to me, every time your face
glimpses mine it doesn't seem to have to smile

the eyes are enough.

<u>Untitled [I miss you every day]</u>

I miss you everyday
even in the expanse of years that are sure to come
where I may only glimpse you,
running from noise to noise
to drown out the thought of you sitting and looking out your window
seeing how many stars reflect the face of me,
(somewhere off, a plucked feather dipped in the ink of the sky,
writing the words I am writing now)

All I can say is I hope you are smiling
I hope I find you
I hope I can learn your name

First Leaf

Broken, your face in my mind, from dances to walks and phrases.
Emptiness this blackened hole which I thought I saw,
Filled now with blood and smiles and years past
You reach out. You were always bold, you spoke your mind.
With a nail and a scalpel, my chest is split open on the autopsy table
And I grip the table for some sort of justification, some rationalization
Some thought to make it all better for me,
The only comfort being in all these words and tears,
Love was in your heart the whole time.

Trout

Sitting alone in a clouded park
I contemplate your eyes
With gentle pulse of a river
And the fish that are your thoughts
All of them are bright and happy
Because they are alive.

Estranged

a dream in which two colors swirl
pretends to talk about
something
we dare not talk about

looking through valleys and rivers
we wait for the sky stretched canvas
to be painted black

in our loneliness
each star is a whispered prayer
for the painter to just give up already.

Thoughts of Morning

On the grass, under a tree
That great monument of space and time,
I sit, hair and shirt disheveled
Eyes half closed
And hear
Laughter, loud and piercing, in the distance.
I cannot see the culprits.
I don't think that if I was standing right next to them
I could ever see them, and talk to them.
For as I am now, the wind cradles each individual branch,
Occasional eruptions of pure static accompanying
Calls hidden throughout the earth
Where there is no complication
Only pattern
Seen joyfully
As the bird feeds her young
In the shade before sunrise

Cult-ure

Pixels. Images. Plastic covering death-in-a-box
For three payments of

Green grass bends
A fox whips his tail

Auto tuned broadcasters droning censored script
Biodegradable casket. Fabric. Nothing but the

White washed tombs. Falsity is a breath away.
Flip sides, twist and knot. Voila!

A tree glows red. The nature created surrounding us.
Quiet stillness invades your bones. Fall to earth.
And look up at the sun between the trees

<u>Frame</u>

To lightly shake, and reassemble yourself on a PM sleep craze
Dumps a load of penmanship illegible onto the page.

Today was a nightmare of silent nightmares.

                              No Connection.

          And what am I?

Sometimes I think we are all colored puzzle pieces.
And at the end
The pieces will fit, and smile back at you.

Flowers

Pot on my windowsill
The sufferings, hopes and dreams
Of a young boy half his age

Taken through dirty streets
But left all those with painted faces
And so, let them pass.

Broken slowly along the people that he had distanced through the days,
the sun that wasn't there, and the flowers that did not open

Why can't your flower open?

Praying that a tree would be weak and pliable
So that I may be young again

For the branches were made for sitting beneath
And falling leaves a veil from the destruction beyond.
Shelter from the sweat and toil of life

The hollow, shattered orbs of youth
With just as much a heart

It's a shame
After all these years, the flower was a rose.

Words

The word trust rang in the room
It sprung up the few who had slipped the dark corners of his mind
to the casual passerby.

Safety was the pool floats,
and a boy that had drowned in the river hidden in the woods

Love was insistent, no honey, take the seat, I'll run and get the car
Out in the rain which produced a grey shade to the world,

Some muck, that he was willing to step in, getting his shoes muddy on the way
As his grey trousers darkened, and his shirt stuck to his skin,
He thought without any restraint,

The stanza for all the years of the past,
Ringing out in what he spoke me to me now, as we were alone,
Giving stories from our lives set in simple phrases of wisdom,

This spoke above them all
Giving reason for all things before it
I love you.

Failure

you told me all the things you couldn't tell others
tales of broken glass and piss, fist cratered drywall
and the sanctuary of pillows and blankets

there are no lights on
your whispering in the dark
makes me feel whole

as if I'm taking something
which was set down long ago
bringing you a step closer to a cathartic hum
of Buddhist monks surrounded
by a canopy of trees.

but as I sit with you on the floor
legs folded, breathing slowed, I realize

this is not you reaching inner peace
but you running out naked

arms covered in blood
chanting your past to each apartment door
leaving your bandages and shawl at home.

Trees outline a shadow against a dark sky. Weightless, inattentive – images, lights, and memories. With every quickened step step step I transfer my troubles to the ground beneath me – agony, anger, sorrow – now immersed in pavement and gravel, gone from my troubled mind. I now notice the air (cool, unmoving presence, pushed only by the swing and clutch of my fingers) and the bend of leaves on moon silver shade. For this I walk in the night, alone.

<u>On you surrounded by my friends who I do not know.</u>

I look at you now
Honestly saying that here is no one I have ever loved
or hated more than you, a soul dragging at your ankles
The moon reflecting off you, making you who you are
(the only object that has done so in all the years I gazed with you)

Knowing nothing but wishing for every warmth in the world
But never getting because deep down
You knew it was worthless.

Slave

Modern terrors
Run through night of nights
Watch a deadened sky
Leap on top of stairways
Through chimneys on Dick van New York
Crawl through screens, lock arms around sleeping children,
And try to squeeze light
Broadcast yourself on All Things Considered
Color yourself in on CNN –
Manifest yourself in green and red neon numbers
With thousands standing under watching with breath poised
In unanswered letters abbreviated, no comments on a rusty pixel board
Traffic accident, monster semi
A charging lion, you,
Armed with a safety pin
Psalms, a velvet sheet soft
Blaring horns, turning signal gone
A violin concerto
See the air and mountains
Us, poor players of our surroundings
Cease your struggle;
Submit   be free.

<u>Cross</u>

i awaken the tinder

flames enveloping

dull newspaper pages,

with quivering psalms

and smile

for the strength that is not mine.

Untitled [Are we all dying?]

Are we all dying?
I said near the foot of my uncle's coffin
He was adorned with a well-ironed sport shirt
Which my father purchased, his skin worn, not his anymore.
The tailor said he would stay open
as long as he needed to make a sale.

The funeral was tomorrow, and father held off buying
The suit until the last moment
Pouring over his brother's possessions
Glancing at old photos only if he could help it
Finishing bottles of wine that his brother
kept for special occasions

Outside it began to rain. The droplets pelted the roof,
falling down glass at the store's entrance
leaving a trail of scars which seemed to curve
in numerous directions
meeting together on the ground
father would walk from one end of the room to the other,
and then stop,
becoming infatuated with the fabrics on display.

Once, he put a black cloth over the gray
shirt that he wore that was still warm.

Stop that I said. Put that down

Father shook himself, resumed his pacing.

The suit was finished.
The owner held it out for my father to take with his pale hands.
He stood there a long time.

In the car, my father threw the suit in the back seat,
quick, violent motion, tossing away the touch of a leper.
We drove in silence through the black night.
The entire world was awash in nothingness,
swirling in some unceasing pattern that I never knew,
would never know, until I died and became a part of it.

My father choked back a sob.
It sounded the plea of a dying animal, which before had been
graceful, free and fast, using all to its glory.
He spoke words that I couldn't hear.
When I did not reply he spoke louder, saying my name.

His voice was broken.   Roll down the windows.

                                                          But dad, it's raining.

He turned, held his face
to all he could not see, bracing himself against it.

I know.

Widowed Chapel

the summer winds
sweep the garden
alone
without help
of the ones who remember

<u>Untitled</u>

In a conversation I had with you
On the telephone
It seems you are running with nothing in your hands
As few simple shadows chasing as you turn
These your own, conjured from childhood
To be crazed for blood and tears,
The only things you have ever known
Until you put on red lipstick with the sunrise glinting off it.

Listening intently to words plainspoken,
I hear you pleading;
You could have been talking of the time of day,
But the notes of your voice play a lamentation for
When everything was simple
You dancing under a summertime sprinkler and laughing
When you loved you

<u>Evolution of Separation</u>

I cannot shake us
Wandering in the words that we grew in
Tracing our fingers through the ruts of necks and shoulders

It's the questions we refuse to ask
That hurt the most;
Will we survive a sunrise together
Nervously waiting to give our eyes and pressing hands a name

I cannot shake you
That's the cursed portion of memory
You are a ghost in my room
Drifting backwards
Until I only see your pupils in the wall

<u>Meditation</u>

So many of us
(the glassy eyed people)
run from image to image

A hologram
For the skin and beating heart

I would much rather be
Quiet, stretched out in the grass
Listening to the gentle rhythms of the trees

Funeral (of a grandmother)

Silence present in the air
As we look silvery hair
And that face that once smiled
Is rigidly held straight, in contrast to her years

We remember a morning dress
Gentle fingers, soft caress
Some eggs in the morning, with footsteps on the floor

Try to think of aging
Slowly, the seconds passing by
Waiting to turn your hair to grey

Try to think of loving
With a light in the living room
Words withstood the test of time

Try to think of eyelids closed
Oh! Orbs once gleaming strong and bright
Learning, teaching from day until night
Now curtained over to keep out the light

We knew where her road would lead
For those who bless do not truly bleed
Is a flower, wilted, still a flower?
All the minutes lived, and smiling hours?

Servant Memory nods his head
All the dead are not truly dead
They all whisper in our ear
Each to their appointed, when the time is right.

<u>Night-time</u>

i do not know
where I came from
this mixture of substances
called me
does not know why its here.
i've been for so long
i still feel like a toddler
a lost, confused, angry body
craving simple delight.

what is it that makes us
twist in bed sheets
slap our toes to the floor
and say hello to the morning

each of us thinks there is something or someone
waiting for us outside the door
or lying beside us in bed.

that eyes wide light tells us more
than clenched shut darkness can.

maybe that's the difference
between the sleeping and the dead
hope and despair
getting up and staying in.

Orange

i watch you
eat an orange
lovingly, quietly
flesh tearing
beneath your will

i am sad
for the orange

slowly
it becomes
a part of you.

Seventh Realm

in my worst fantasy and best nightmare
i am in my coffin and i am awake.

i stare at the walls.
they seem vaginal
a new beginning for my traveller mind,
trembling at the threshold of what is reality
and what is dream in my sleep which is death

the writing on the inside of my coffin
tells me to push
on the sides, break free
from my self imposed exile.

so i tear
the coffin
from it corners

        leave, drifting to

                  alone

          stars
    silence.

Acknowledgements

It was very much a pleasure to write this book, but none of it could have been done without a select group of very special people in my life. I'll thank all of you in chronological order.

(Obviously) to Mom and Dad. Thank you for standing behind me in each of my endeavors, even the failures. Thanks go especially to Dad for getting the idea of a book off the ground, despite my firm cynicism and self-doubt in regards to my work. Dr. Drown, thank you for giving me the love of good literature and critical analysis skills to separate the dross from the wheat. Lewis and Tolkien all the way! Mr. Vailes, for sitting down and looking at the drafts of my early stages, as well as our conversations on what it means to be an artist, and how not to waste time. To Mrs. Barbara Fowler, for first letting me know my potential as a poet and a writer. To Dr. Molly Coffman, for furthering my poetic abilities and being critical of me when my pride got in the way. I'd like to thank James Cherry, Frank X. Walker, and Bobby Rogers. And finally, thanks to the Union Trailblazer for first publishing *Untitled [Are we all dying?]* and *Funeral (of a Grandmother)*.

www.ingramcontent.com/pod-product-compliance
Lightning Source LLC
Chambersburg PA
CBHW031208090426

42736CB00009B/834